Page 06

D1549828

Page 48

Contents

Page 20

First published in Great Britain in 2002 by Fourth Estate
A Division of HarperCollinsPublishers
77-85 Fulham Palace Road, London W6 8JB
www.4thestate.com

Copyright © Zeppotron Ltd 2002

10 9 8 7 6 5 4 3 2 1

The right of Charlie Brooker to be identified as the author of this
work has been asserted by him in accordance with the Copyright,
Designs and Patents Act 1988

A catalogue record for this book is available from the British Library

ISBN 1-84115-730-9

Written by Charlie Brooker, Ben Caudell, Peter Holmes, Neil
Webster, Simon Swatman and Jonathan Blyth. Added pixel
mangling by Milo Waterfield and Mara Goes. Thanks to Paul
Gilheany, Debra Evans, Andy Miller and all at 4th Estate and M2,
David Miller, Tanya Bruwer, Charlotte Lloyd, Roz Kerr, Juliet Burke,
Steph and Ol, Richie and Bridget, Sarah Hedley, Christine Carty,
Mallo, Macca, and everyone else.

Book design by M2: Tony Lyons, Duncan Youel,
David Edgell, Philippa Baile, Kate Stretton,
Lynnette Eve, Tain Oliff. Illustrations by Tony McSweeney.

Printed and bound in Italy by Editorial Johnson Ltd

Page 49

Everyday use

Spoons. Kettles. Alarm clocks. Toasters. Switchblades. There are some gadgets that prove so utterly indispensable, you simply have to use them every day. And that's precisely what this collection of gizmos is. Are. Is?

But make no mistake – although they may be designed for use "every day", there's nothing "every day" about them! We're confident these products will leave you whirling with amazement each time you so much as approach them! And there's not many household items you can say that about – for instance, when was the last time you jerked with astonishment at, say, a common-or-garden spoon? Unless you saw one being pushed up a wolf's arse on the internet or something.

These widgets and devices will change your life forever. In fact, you'll wonder how you ever managed without them. And if you break or lose them, you'll probably kill yourself.*

Christmas Special!
Eliminate Christmas dinner guilt
with this ultra-pampered fowl.

Little Lord Turkey (page 11)

* For which we take no responsibility.

The alarm clock that demands your full attention

Nobody likes having to get out of bed in the morning – especially at the behest of a mere alarm clock. It's a sad fact that many of us are capable of sleeping straight through even the most insistent "wake up" noises, simply because we have scant respect for the device that is causing them. The result? Unexpected lie-ins, poor timekeeping records and head-on crashes on the way to the office.

Now, thanks to the Facial Stabbing Alarm Clock, such problems are a thing of the past. First it jolts you awake with an ear-cracking siren, then it starts counting down from ten. If you're still in bed by the time it reaches one, it'll stab you repeatedly about the face and neck with a razor-sharp kitchen knife! We guarantee you'll be out of the bedroom like a shot, bang on time each and every morning!

The Facial Stabbing Alarm Clock £209.99

everyday use 03

The pocket hand-expansion bee that helps you appease Chad Michaels, Woodland God

Chad Michaels. The name strikes fear into the hearts of all who have witnessed his fury or heard tales of his legendary wrath. Villages destroyed. Churches smashed to rubble by an unseen hand. Farmhands split asunder, their twitching entrails draped hideously across their shoulders like the grotesque tendrils of an obscene meat octopoid. What can be done to appease this terrible woodland deity?

According to the Book of Revelations, only the sight of an oversized palm can quell His anger. Until recently, prosthetic hands were used to distract Chad Michaels, but their effect was only temporary, and merry hell quickly followed. Now, thanks to the GrowBee 2000, a silver insect kissed by a dying gypsy, your hand can expand to over four times its normal size – and stay there – provided you keep it in a breast pocket and repeatedly rub it with the opposing hand while fixing your eyes on the horned God before you. Rub the bee. Rub the bee. Keep rubbing the bee or damn your eyes, your life is ashes. YOUR LIFE IS ASHES.

GrowBee 2000 Hand-Expansion Bee £2999.99

Above: view as seen by the internal PocketCam

everyday use 05

At last – instant spousal chastisement enters the digital age

Women! Until now, to maintain the upper hand in any relationship you've had to rely on your innate ability to remember and log your partner's transgressions, recalling from memory the most insignificant of annoyances, then meticulously dissecting them in excruciating, mindfucking detail. But all that's about to change.

With NagMaster 2000, those days are long gone.

This simple software application allows you to compile every minuscule blunder into an extensive database of acrimony, giving you argument-winning bitter recriminations at the click of a mouse. Was it August the 3rd last year that he muttered something disparaging about your sister? You know it was, and now you have spreadsheet proof.

NagMaster 2000 makes spousal chastisement less demanding than ever! Every argument, every dispute, every spat is yours for the taking. And there is nothing men can do except apologise from within the fog of their own bewilderment.

NagMaster 2000 £49.99

Shred your books inside this gleaming metallic athlete's head

How many times have you finished a novel, then longed to shred the entire book inside a chrome athlete's head? Thanks to the very latest in shredding technology, that dream is now a reality. This metal Olympian stands poised in the throes of athletic endeavour, a peerless example of physical perfection, while concealed within his cranium are twenty-nine razor-sharp rotating steel blades. Simply feed your book into the skull-top thresher, then relax as the whirling cutters shred your tome. Grisham, Dickens, stories about horses or camping – the shredder pulps all fictions without discrimination, and makes book storage worries a thing of the past.

Those who say a bookcase makes an attractive addition to any room simply haven't seen our shredder in action! From the moment the athlete's cutters whirr and grind within his metal head, and the teeth begin to chomp and chew novels to mush, you'll wonder why you ever thought shelves were an option.

Athlete Book Shredder: £29.99

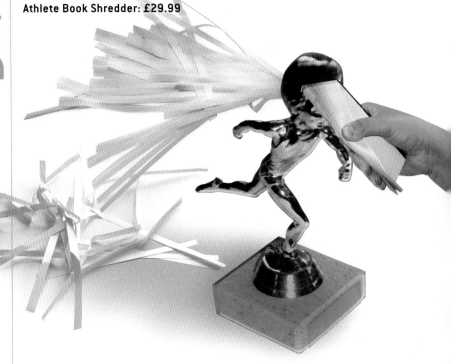

The cycling monkey that provides an ironic counterpoint to your apparently limitless misery

Bellowing your lungs out with absolute despair. It's a state of mind we can all identify with, particularly if we're feeling lost, or lonely, or we've just banged our elbow on that bloody doorframe for the third time this morning.

If you're in the mood for a little primal screaming, here's a clever gadget that will make the most of your vocal outpourings. It's a mechanical monkey on a tricycle powered by your desolate howling. Simply bellow down the attached pipe, and the louder and more anguished your cries, the faster the little fellow pedals. Round and round and round he goes, dementedly circling the room while you heave up all the pain.

It won't help ease your misery, but will make it appear somehow more poignant to anyone looking on (be they observing you through a window, a crack in the door, or perhaps via some kind of as-yet-uninvented surveillance device made out of a genetically engineered eyeball on the end of a grisly length of spine, bound into place with a grotesque plait together with veins and sinew).

• Particularly useful for single mums: kids will be too busy gurgling with joy at the sight of the pedalling monkey to become traumatised by accompanying parental despair.

• Requires no batteries – relies on screaming alone.

• Available with fez, top hat, or hilarious propeller beanie (pictured).

Despair–Fuelled Cycling Monkey £199.99

everyday use 07

Put yourself in control by seceding from the United Kingdom of Great Britain and Northern Ireland

Where does the Government of the United Kingdom get off? Raking billions from your pay packet to give gypos a free ride?! Telling you what you can and can't do in your own home?! Basically force-feeding your kids with drugs and limp-wristed, do-gooding ideals?! Who the hell do they think they are, other than the democratically elected rulers of the British Isles?

Well now's the chance to get your own back. Previously it was simply too expensive to secede from the UK – but this handy pack contains everything you need to legally declare yourself (and your loved ones) an independent nation state: republic, dictatorship, or monarchy – at last it's up to you!

It couldn't be simpler. Assembled by a team of world-class constitutional lawyers, this pack contains all the paperwork you need, including a detailed refutation of the 1688 Treaty of Settlement, an opt-out of the 1707 Act of Union, a letter to send to the local council, a flag and a crown. Simply sign and date each form – it's as simple as writing a will – and hey presto. If Rhodesia can do it so can you!

This watertight documentation* should technically result in you being declared your own sovereign state, with absolute autonomous power over yourself. Just imagine what you could do: Abolish taxes! Invade other countries! Throw out the immigrants! Foster a more enlightened attitude to man-boy relationships! Erect as tall a fence as you want! Import foodstuffs and coal! Sign a treaty with Poland – then tear it up and dance around laughing! Become an international pariah! Develop weapons of mass destruction! Bid for the World Cup! Print your own currency! Sign extradition treaties! Become a haven for terrorist organisations! Stand in the middle of the road cupping your nuts in a soup ladle! You might as well – you can do anything you want because for once YOU'RE in charge – not those so-called "experts" from City Hall!

Be Your Own Country Kit £14,999.00
*As yet untested in court.

Who says women can't be reduced to mere numbers?

Here's a must for all red-blooded males: the Lothario's Abacus, the world's premier device for helping you calculate precisely how many naked female parts you've seen in your lifetime. Simply use your memory to reel through past sexual encounters, slide the corresponding beads along each time you recall seeing a breast, buttock or mimsy, and hey presto: lasting mathematic proof of your success with women – a set of cold, hard numbers you'll cherish *forever!*

Lothario's Abacus £29.99

everyday use

09

2000 handy functions – in a single rock!

Paperweight or primitive weapon? The choice is yours! This versatile rock has literally thousands of uses. Break seashells, scuff garage doors, knock loved ones unconscious, or simply place it on a table and flick rice at it all afternoon! It's up to you, and it's all right here – in a rock!

OmniRock £199.99

Let BrainCement™ slow anguish to a manageable level

Everyone worries from time to time. Perhaps the world situation looks grimmer than usual, or a close relative has died. Or maybe you're upset because you've got a face like a rucksack full of dented bells and pretty girls won't kiss you. Whatever the cause, the end result is always the same: lying awake at night, tormented by your own thoughts, your mind engaging in hand-to-hand combat with the forces of psychological desolation.

Now at last there's a way to slow the ceaseless rush of negative contemplation: BrainCement™ – the mental retardant you simply inject directly into your mind. Simply fill the handy syringe

applicator and inject the BrainCement™ into your ear, or, if you really couldn't give a toss any more, into your tear duct. Within minutes the clever BrainCement™ makes your brain solidify, leaving it as blissfully useless as a chunk of solid rock – for up to 48 hours!

BrainCement™ £4.99

All-new six-nozzle set including the fantastic lachrymal duct blocker absolutely free!

Do not use while operating heavy machinery, appearing in a circus, or overseeing the day-to-day affairs of The United States of America.

The guilt-free Christmas turkey that spends its final days in unprecedented luxury

Everyone loves Christmas, with its spirit of giving, rekindling of old friendships, and hypocritical exchange of token gifts with detested family members. The single downside is the turkey – we all savour the taste of its flesh melting slowly in our hot, wet little mouthholes, but who hasn't experienced a twinge of guilt at the thought that until recently it was happily pecking corn, only to be silenced mid-gobble by its own murder.

Now guilt-free Christmas fowl has finally arrived, with Little Lord Turkey. Living the ultimate playboy lifestyle, your chosen bird spends its final days fed on only the finest of foods, drinking vintage wine, smoking cigars and snorting lines of purest cocaine, jetting from one exclusive showbiz party to the next in the back of a Lear jet wreathed in pearls and honey – altogether pampered in a manner you could only dream of, right until the moment a cold-fingered farmhand snaps its neck like a feathered fucking breadstick and you hack up the body and lob the pieces down your throat.

Little Lord Turkey £24.99

Little Lord Turkey's itinerary of decadence

Day One

Turkey arrives at Bellingham Hall, the sumptuous country residence of the Earl of Godfrey, to begin its week-long stay in the lap of luxury.

To help our feathered friend unwind after a tiring journey, a trained masseuse kneads its wings, world-famous aromatherapist Theodore Gresp wafts a gentle bouquet of pine needles and black cherries beneath its beak, and legendary DJ duo Coldcut drop an exclusive ambient chill-down set designed specifically to lull our anxious fowl into a deep and tranquil sleep.

Day Two

The turkey awakes to breakfast in bed: sixteen generous handfuls of gourmet Belgian feed and a glass of freshly-squeezed orange juice.

Having browsed the morning papers, our guest is carried into the "Palace of Pecks" – a cavernous hallway filled with interesting objects to mindlessly knock one's beak against.

Refined afternoon entertainment comes courtesy of the Kronos Quartet, followed by croquet and cocktails in the evening.

Day Three

A day of Bacchanalian decadence for our lucky bird, which begins with it being awoken by an attractive gigolo gently performing cunnilingus while simultaneously stroking the back of its neck.

Having been lapped to climax, the satiated turkey enjoys a relaxing smoke while watching the latest Hollywood blockbusters on a state-of-the-art surround-sound digital widescreen DVD home-cinema system.

It is then tongued back to shuddering orgasm after shuddering orgasm until it can cluck no more.

Day Four

Rock and Roll! Turkey awakes to yet more oral pleasuring, before being drip-fed a heady cocktail of sparkling wine and top-grade cocaine.

A quick live set from Blur on the lawn of Bellingham Hall, then it's off by helicopter to a trendy London nightclub, where an evening of dancing, mayhem and yet more drugs and cunnilingus awaits.

Bird ends the night on a luxury coach, eating canapés and having cocaine blown up its arse by a male model while a hardcore pornographic film in which a George Clooney lookalike rubs his penis against a turkey's cheek plays on a massive overhead screen.

Day Five

Turkey shaken awake by vigorous plucking. Neck broken by grinning farmhand. Guts removed by mechanical suction device. Lifeless cadaver hurled in back of van and driven direct to your door.

Merry Christmas.

Gadgets + technology

Wondering whether the future's arrived yet? What are you, mad? Take a look outside the window: sliding doors and happy pills as far as the eye can see.

Keep up with the white-hot cutting-edge of up-to-the-minute gadgetology with the following selection of high-tech helpers that are **GUARANTEED** to push you kicking and screaming right over the forefront of tomorrow's frontier.

All our electronic goods are built to the highest standards by a team of robots in a futuristic factory on the Moon* before being shipped to you on a 21st-century jet bike ridden by a woman with purple hair.

Your next-door-neighbours will turn green with envy as they struggle with their antiquated wooden implements while you nonchalantly juggle the most sophisticated technological thingery the modern world has to offer.

But don't worry about that now! Stop reading and start buying! After all, it's your future!

Guaranteed to annoy the accountant in your life. A bit.

Puerile Calculator (page 20)

We reserve the right to use a sweatshop in Doncaster instead.

The truly barbaric way to relieve executive stress

It's tough at the top – tough, hard and cruel. Being a high-ranking business executive does have its rewards – astronomical wages, widespread respect, mind-blowing power, and near-constant sexual congress with a string of glamorous partners who wouldn't stoop down to rub shit on your nose were it not for your status – but these bonuses are scant reward for the gnawing stress that accompanies the job.

Squeeze-balls and undersized basketball hoops are all very well, but the surest way to alleviate tension is to cause unbearable physical distress to another living creature. The product of fifteen years of sinister research, the BioShriek PainCow is a miniature bovine genetically engineered to suffer at your bequest. Encased within a perspex dome, the doe-eyed beast is fastened to the spot via an intricate network of tendril-like sinews which carry spasms of excruciating torment to every nerve centre in its body at the touch of a button. Worried about the Dow Jones? Take it out on the PainCow. Lost that takeover bid? Hit the switch and watch its tiny flank shiver with agony until its udders squirt blood. Suffering impotence? Bang that nub and it'll wail in cow language until your penis hardens to a stump of hot, fat oak. Way to go, boss! *Way to go!*

BioShriek PainCow £499.99

The television that launches hot, wet clumps of real human shit into your stupid fucking face

Television. Once hailed as the most sophisticated medium in the history of mankind, these days it's little more than a parade of ceaseless electronic idiocy, cynically pandering to the basest desires of the lowest common denominator. For all the good it does you, it might as well hurl shit into your face while you watch it. And now it does.

This state-of-the-art set comes complete with a high-velocity waste-firing gun bolted onto the side, capable of firing clump after clump of warm brown shit directly into the eyes of whichever gormless simpleton happens to be sitting passively before it morning, noon and night, gawping blankly ahead like an inanimate glove puppet, scarcely able to notice the relentless damp slap of thick, sticky shit splattering against their cheeks, the choking stench of effluence dribbling down their lips, or the increasing rigidity as it hardens around them like clay in the sunshine, slowly transforming them into an immobile auburn statue. Order yours now. And keep it tuned to ITV.

Shit-Flinging Television £299.99

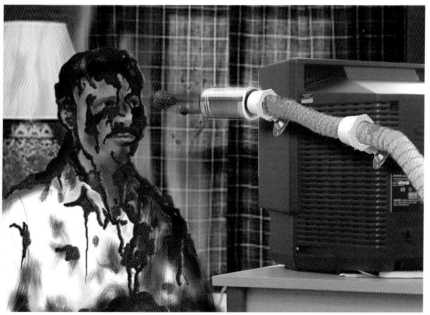

Could this be the world's cosiest noose?

As anyone who's hung themselves can't tell you, ordinary rope nooses may be effective at snapping your neck like a desiccated pencil, but they're also scratchy and uncomfortable, often leaving the user with painful friction burns and irritated skin – which means your relatives won't be the only ones with something to cry about when you take that ultimate plunge.

Here's the solution – the SnugDrop Deluxe Noose. Your neck will love being cuddled by its quilted, lavender-scented surface, while minuscule speakers hidden in the knot play a selection of soothing panpipe music to bid you farewell as you dangle off to deadland. The comfortable appearance also disguises an efficient killing machine: a high-tensile steel hoop buried deep within ensures a clean, efficient break the moment you step off that chair. It's by far the comfiest way to wave goodbye to everything – we guarantee you'll think it's so cosy, it's almost worth living for! Almost.

SnugDrop Deluxe Noose £199.99

The high-tech alarm that protects your family from inevitable paedophile intrusion

It's every parent's nightmare: one minute their child is enjoying harmless fun in the family garden, the next they're being chased round and round the picnic table by a drooling sex offender. So what can be done to prevent these sickening maniacs?

The answer is Paedo-Go – the world's first lawn-mounted pederast alarm. Sleek and unobtrusive, it screams into life the instant it detects the electronic tag of a nearby convicted sexual deviant, thereby alerting you and your family to imminent fuckdanger.

Simply choose from the four pre-set alarm tones (dispassionate robot, bellowing yokel, gunfire, or furious lynch mob), place the device in "standby" mode, and bingo: you can relax in the knowledge that your children are entirely safe, unless one day butchered by your own hand in an inexplicable act of senseless rage.

Paedo-Go £40,404.99

gadgets & technology 19

Puerile Calculator makes light work of geek tormentation

This state-of-the-art electronic gadget has been specially designed to mildly irritate nerds of all ages. No matter how hard you hammer away at the keys, the display remains the same: the word "TOSSER" spelt out in bold, stark capitals. Sort of sums it all up, really.

Puerile Calculator £79.99

Which route is quickest? As The Crow Flies, of course!

Who needs expensive in-car navigation computers, with their smug LCD monitors and know-it-all satellite location systems? As The Crow Flies is the economical solution to all your course-plotting needs. Essentially a large fixed arrow on the dashboard that always points forwards, As The Crow Flies will direct you to the shortest route possible without smashing your wallet to pieces in the process.

Indication enthusiasts!
As The Crow Flies
can also be removed and used for pointing at things, including:

- Picturesque hills
- Attractive sunbathers
- Chalk formations
- House keys
- John Nettles
- Quizzical looks
- Other arrows

... and many, many more

As The Crow Flies £69.99

Caution: when using **As The Crow Flies** for in-car navigation, care must be taken to retain the use of eyes, as the system itself will not alert driver to potential obstacles such as rivers, cul de sacs, pedestrians, multiplex cinemas and oncoming cars.

Headgear

The human head is an incredibly versatile thing: it can be used for talking, remembering, eating, thinking, and scanning crowds for potential miscreants.

And let's not overlook its greatest function: it makes an ideal resting place for a hat. But don't just settle for any old hat: over the next few pages you'll find examples of the highest-tech headgear around – state-of-the-art gadgetry you can take anywhere you can fit your head.

The sun has got his hat on… and now*, so have you!

Enjoy full-blown lunacy – at the touch of a button!

Schizophrenia Helmet
(page 24)

* Assuming you buy something

Before

After

It's time to eradicate the poor

As every affluent citizen knows, tramps are the cancer of our streets. Whether you're queuing for the cashpoint, climbing from a cab, or window-shopping for diamonds and gold, there's always a beggar selfishly wallowing in his own urine and misery nearby. Now you can be rid of their unsightly poverty with the Pauper-B-Gone virtual reality helmet.

The Pauper-B-Gone's unique Retina Distraction system instantly replaces scenes of pavement squalor with cheerful depictions of cartoon animation. Is that a broken soul belching cider through his nose while pathetically begging for tuppence outside the launderette? Not any more – now it's loveable *Papa Smurf* enjoying a jug of *Smurf juice* and cheerfully *Smurfing a song about Smurfland!*

Each helmet comes with three variable poverty filters, allowing you to select the precise level of hardship you wish to ignore. Choose from: "cold, bleeding and fingerless", "Scottish" or "a touch of the council". With the Pauper-B-Gone VR helmet you need never so much as glance at a piece of pavement shit again.

Pauper-B-Gone Poverty Concealment Helmet £899.99

Enjoy television to the full – without troublesome powers of reason!

Millions of Britons watch television for hour after hour, each and every night – but there are some who find they aren't capable of following suit. The ceaseless parade of soulless posturing, leering sensationalism and feeble-minded pantomime which entertains the rest of the nation simply leaves them cold. The problem? Excessive use of the thought process is preventing them from settling down and enjoying TV's knuckleheaded shenanigans without question.

Help is at hand in the form of the Auto-Lobotomising TV Hat – a stylish and comfortable piece of headgear, complete with its own drill which hangs from the front and pierces your forehead, skewering your brain in seconds. As the diamond-tipped drill bit churns your mind into slush, you'll be able to concentrate fully on the on-screen antics, in the docile manner you're supposed to. Welcome back to the herd, Mr. Sheep, welcome back.

Auto-Lobotomising TV Hat £2339.99

headgear

23

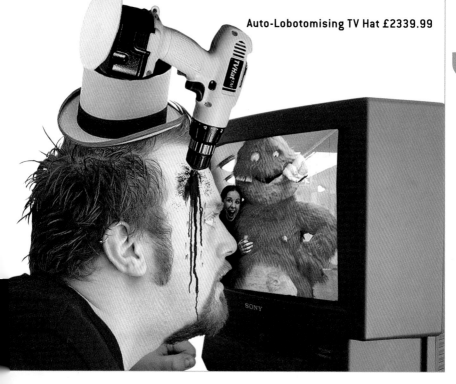

All the fun of schizophrenia – in a hat!

Genuine, full-blown madness is a double-edged sword – on the one hand there's the bliss of total freedom from responsibility and continual audio-visual stimulation. On the other, the misery of continual bewilderment and meaningless despair. You simply couldn't experience one without the other until now.

Developed by a team of psychological engineers, the Schizophrenia Helmet is the easy way to experience the zany world of unfettered madness. Accusatory voices whisper through side-mounted headphones into your ear, while high-tech eyeglasses project an unending stream of disturbing imagery directly into your corneas. Within seconds you'll be sweating, screaming and glancing left and right, your face contorted into a grotesque mask of horror and confusion. When it gets too much – simply switch off and plunge back into reality. And with adjustable settings for the strength and intensity of voices and visions, it's as versatile as it's stylish. *Not for sale to children or handgun enthusiasts or both.*

Schizophrenia Helmet £499.99

headgear 25

Could this be the world's most dramatically effective baker-infuriating hat?

Bakers. With their beady eyes, callow expressions and nauseating interest in dough, they inspire disgust in us all. But until now the process of actively expressing one's revulsion has been fraught with complication. Vocal insults get lost amongst the din of oven doors and cake trays, while abusive gesticulation is often mistaken for affectionate mime.

This lightweight, unisex hat sends a clear message to anybody employed in the baking industry thanks to a prominent magnetic placard that includes a set of ten pre-scripted slogans, including "All Bread is Shit", "I Piss on Yeast" and the disarmingly forthright "Fuck All Bakers, Fuck Their Friends, Fuck Their Families, and Fuck Everyone Who Knows Them". Whenever this headgear makes an appearance, the tears of an enraged pastry whore raining down upon the patisserie counter are sure to follow. Deluxe version also fires tear gas, razor blades and dog shit directly into their cunt baker faces.

Baker-Baiting Hat £39.99

Convince imaginary whores your face is a shop with this clever head-mounted disguise

Wherever you look, there they are. Tiny illusory whores, striding around in their cheap clothes, soaked head to toe in sick perfumes, plying their shameful miniature trade in the most insulting manner possible. Clearly they must be stopped – and here's how.

This ingenious facial camouflage kit transforms your head into a persuasive replica of an ordinary newsagent's shop. The tough plastic awning conceals your furious eyes without blocking your view of their undersized wrongdoing, while a realistic newspaper rack and advertising placard squat either side of your open mouth, causing it to resemble a welcoming retailer's door. In the arrogant harlots stroll – some perhaps are whistling or combing their awful hair. Others perhaps are not. You pause a moment, mouth agape.

Then gobble them up! That's it! Gobble them, gobble them, stinkholes and all! Tee hee!

Hallucinatory Prostitute Retail Bewilderment Mask £34.99

26 headgear

Corrections

Two wrongs don't make a right. And one wrong doesn't make a right either. But there's nothing wrong with exercising your right to right wrongs, right? In this section of our catalogue you'll find a range of products dedicated to correcting errors of all kinds, from wonky shelves* to wayward children.

Whether you want to use them separately, or in conjunction with each other, or one at a time over a particularly gruelling Bank Holiday weekend, the following gizmos and widgets and gadgets and items and objects and things will help turn your world from a twirling bauble of errortude into a sparkling mass of just-so nice-nice.

Sick of the neighbours?
Turn them into ducks!

The Cursed Headdress of Perzang (page 32)

* Actually, we don't
have anything for shelves.

The uncompromising talking bear that renders pleasant father – child relationships impossible

It's a situation every divorced or separated mum will recognise instantly – the weekend is looming, and it's the absent father's turn with your child. Cue two days of covert brainwashing, as he drags your innocent offspring round theme parks, zoos, and football matches, plying them with endless sweets and gifts in a desperate bid to make himself look like a halfway decent dad Well, no. No. It shall not be.

Scupper his chances with Mr. Chocolate – the talking bear that skillfully undermines

your ex-partner's charm offensive with a selection of apt phrases designed to shatter your child's confidence in that no-good runaround father of theirs. From whispered aspersions regarding his affections, to bold outright dismissals of his worth as a human being, Mr. Chocolate enables you to sustain a vice-like grip on your child's affections even as they enter the mind-mangling clutches of that lying, two-faced piece of shit arsehole who couldn't keep his pea-sized wang in his pants if it was stapled to his adulterous thigh.

Mr. Chocolate Talking Bear £69.99

Say "bye bye" to earplugs – and "hello" to the use of Tongue Destroyer

Noisy neighbours? Nagging spouse? Tyrannical boss? Now you can silence them all – *permanently* – with these handy soluble tablets. Simply slip one into their favourite drink, and within seconds of consumption their tongue will dissolve completely, leaving them blissfully mute for life.

Tongue Destroyer (pack of 24 tablets) £89.99

Caution: Do not accidentally shov tablets into your own eyes.

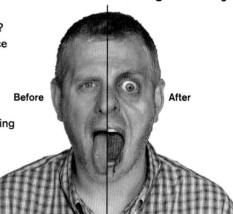

Before

After

Remove awkward notions from your child's head at a stroke

Look at your child. Go on, stare it in the eye. The fruit of your loins, the apple of your eye, the whole of your world. Maybe unplanned, maybe unwanted, maybe utterly unloved. But you look after it, you care for it, you put food on the table. And yet all the time it may be secretly laughing at you, ridiculing you, belittling you – by thinking things. Things you don't like. Things you don't want them to think.

It might be thinking about Islam, or death, or going outside, or taking sandwiches to the poor, or love, or the pity of war, or physical pleasure, or how much it hates you, or any amount of crazy stuff you're not happy with. If only there was a way you could stop it. Well now you can!

Until now it's been prohibitively expensive to find out if your child has been thinking ideas, let alone to remove them forever. Chinese torture techniques have had some success in this area, but are currently illegal and can stain. But now the remarkable ThinkGozer™ can permanently remove surplus thoughts, ideas and desires in just a few brief, painful seconds.

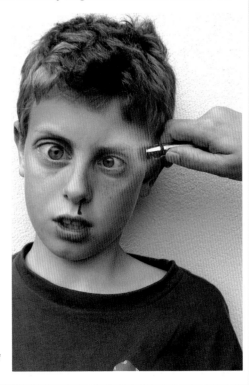

It works by sending an ultra-sound blast into your child's brain to burn away the nodes infected with unwanted thoughts. Just place it next to the temple, switch it on and keep it there until you can detect no trace of dissent in their eyes. No mess, no fuss – *just simple power over the thoughts of another.*

• Sound and odour free
• Can remove awkward memories
• Also works on cows

ThinkGozer £29.97

corrections

29

The intelligent underwear that spies on a daughter's desires

She's sixteen. She's your daughter. As far as you're concerned, she's still "daddy's little girl". But there comes a time in every female life when local boys will set her heart a-flutter, causing an irrevocable split in the cherished father-daughter dynamic.

Until now it's been impossible to ascertain precisely when the fine line between harmless romance and raw passion has been breached. These high-tech knickers are the solution. Tiny intelligent microfibres woven into the crotch react on contact with heat and moisture, activating a remote communications device that alerts you to the danger, enabling you to pinpoint the precise moment your angelic offspring sheds her virginal mindset and starts hungering for defilement at the hands and penis of some feral-faced schoolmate.

At last you can confront her with your suspicions, safe in the knowledge that while her mouth may lie, *biology has betrayed the despicable truth* – as surely as though she'd crept into your bedroom in the middle of the night and whispered "Daddy, I'm wet" in your ear.

Incrimiknickers (pack of 6) £44.99

Could this be the world's most entertaining dog execution DVD?

Tying a noose round a dog's neck and hanging it from a bridge is the cool craze that's sweeping the nation – and now you can join in the fun in your living room with this laugh-packed DVD. Containing over ninety minutes of hound-dangling action from across Britain, HangDog Mania will have you and your family in stitches. It's "Dog-Gone" crazy!

Also available:

- Goat Impalation Parade
- Legend of the Badger Guillotine
- Now That's What I Call Sticking a Drill in a Cow's Head
- Horses Aflame!

HangDog Mania £19.99

Harness the powers of an ancient and terrifying elder God

Feeling downtrodden, impotent? Fancy throwing your weight around for a change? With this menacing cursed headdress you can kill absolutely anyone at will – simply by glancing at them!

Fashioned from feathers and the bones of slaughtered wolves, each headdress has been cursed by a dishonoured Tahitian monk. Simply don the headdress, whisper the pre-supplied oath, stare at your intended victim, and blam: they're twice as dead as a dented pram.

KissMammal 2003 User's Manual

Thank you for purchasing the KissMammal 2003 sexual gratification system. Before violating your KissMammal, please read this manual carefully and retain it for future reference.

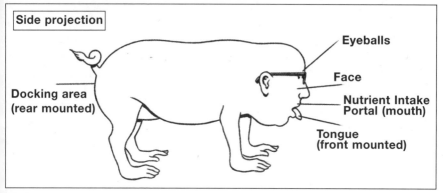

Side projection

Eyeballs
Face
Nutrient Intake Portal (mouth)
Tongue (front mounted)
Docking area (rear mounted)

WARNING To prevent fire or shock hazard, do not push the KissMammal's face into an electrical bar heater while mounting from the rear.

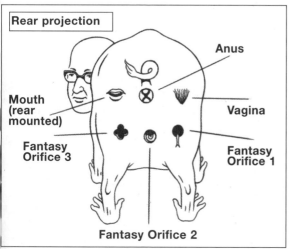

Rear projection

Anus
Mouth (rear mounted)
Vagina
Fantasy Orifice 3
Fantasy Orifice 1
Fantasy Orifice 2

Caution:

Your KissMammal is supplied infection-free. Care should be taken not to share it with other users.

Read carefully before entering your KissMammal.

A few people may experience feelings of intense self-loathing after ejaculating inside a genetically engineered pigbeast. Consult your physician should waves of depression, worthlessness or disgust persist within 48 hours of copulation.

Instructionations

- Do not leave the KissMammal in direct sunlight. Prolonged exposure to the sun may cause orifices to shrivel.

- Store the KissMammal away from children, particularly if you've recently taught it to fellate anything that moves.

- Do not subject the KissMammal to violent physical shock, such as slamming its head in a car door, or kicking it down the stairs and then fucking it.

- Avoid damaging the exterior of the KissMammal with blades or screwdrivers. Additional orifices may be sliced in the flank of the KissMammal, but should always be cauterised within 4 hours.

- Never wrench the KissMammal's spine out and dance around outside your house waving it over your head, shouting "Hey everyone, I just fucked a pig, then pulled this out of its back – ha ha ha". Doing so may lead to social exclusion or criminal proceedings.

Preparing your KissMammal

Your KissMammal arrives vacuum-packed in an airtight plastic pouch. To revive it, simply follow these instructions.

1) Place the packaged KissMammal into a bathtub.

2) Slice open the pouch, discard the covering, and rinse away the saline marinade.

3) Seal bath plughole and run a warm bath as normal, until the unconscious creature is fully immersed.

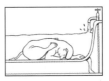

At this point you're free to go and read a book, or perhaps watch a little TV, until the KissMammal is awakened. The resuscitation process should take less than half an hour – you'll be alerted when your new love partner is fully conscious by the sound of it squealing and thrashing about in the tub.

When entering your KissMammal for the first time

Your fuckmonster is likely to become startled during its first sexual encounter, and may start squealing or struggling away from your relentless hammering hips. Calm the appalled beast by stroking the back of its neck or holding a flower against its cheek while whispering in its ear. After initial use, the creature should soon settle down to a lifetime of passive molestation.

KissMammal 2003

Feeding your KissMammal

Thanks to its unique digestion system, the KissMammal can survive simply by ingesting your fluids through any of its six rear-mounted orifices. Excretion occurs discretely in the middle of the night, when the KissMammal will cough up a small number of odourless pellets. Should you wish to encourage the KissMammal to perform traditional defecation on or near your person for the purposes of sexual gratification, simply feed standard cat or dog food into its front-mounted mouth and within twenty minutes a rigid stool will drop from the other end. For more diarrheic movements, which may also be used to lubricate the anal aperture, pour 500ml of olive oil into the KissMammal's throat prior to entry.

Cleaning your KissMammal

Repeated use of the KissMammal is likely to lead to a build-up of coagulated matter, which should be cleaned away to maintain optimum admission. Orifices should be unclogged every three to six weeks using a thumb wrapped in toilet paper (thumbless users may prefer to use a wooden spoon and dishcloth). The outer skin requires less attention since the KissMammal will lick itself clean after each encounter, but should exceptionally heavy build-up of seminal fluid or excrement occur simply place the beast beneath a warm shower for twenty minutes, taking care not to suddenly lose your temper for no reason and slam its head against a tap until its jaw breaks and loads of blood comes out.

Suggested Positions for Enjoying Your KissMammal

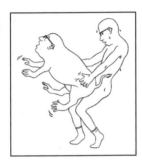

The Backward Farmer

The Lapdog Surprise

The Hammer and Tongs

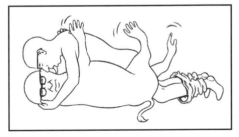

Troublesniping

Can't achieve climax while fornicating with KissMammal?

Some users report initial difficulty in achieving climax while having intercourse with their KissMammal. In such cases the cause is usually psychological: since few people are accustomed to having sex with a writhing manmade jizzjar, it can seem difficult to leap the 'mental gap' required to reach gooey orgasmic bliss. But with a little practice and determination, you can maintain the correct level of mental detachment necessary to sufficiently burst your dyke.

Handy tips include:

- Place the KissMammal's body under a duvet with just the rear end exposed.

- Imagine you're having sex with a Hollywood actress who's preparing for a role as a pig by standing on all fours in your bedroom.

- Stare directly at the orifice you're entering and concentrate on getting it all over with.

- During intercourse, call an unsuspecting female business colleague on the telephone and litter your conversation with oblique references to what you're doing.

KissMammal keeps falling unconscious

Violent or repeated copulation may send your animal into shock, and in extreme cases will lead to loss of consciousness. Should this happen, gently slow your rhythm to maintain a gentle rocking motion while patting the beast gently around the face and coughing politely. If the animal does not regain consciousness within ten minutes, call our customer services helpline.

KissMammal struggles too much

Although designed to be as docile and unquestioning as possible, some KissMammals object to certain forms of sex play. Should such opposition occur, defuse the situation by wedging the KissMammal's head between two heavy objects (such as an armchair and a wall) before proceeding as normal.

KissMammal's orifices are too slack

After prolonged use, your KissMammal's entryholes may start to weaken. Should your enjoyment become impaired, simply order the creature to sit in a bowl of vinegar for 48 hours, smacking it in the face with a broom whenever it tries to get up. If this fails to tighten the entrances, call our customer services helpline and ask about our magic creams.

Flexibility!

Its powers don't end with simple death! With this powerful cursed headdress, you can also...

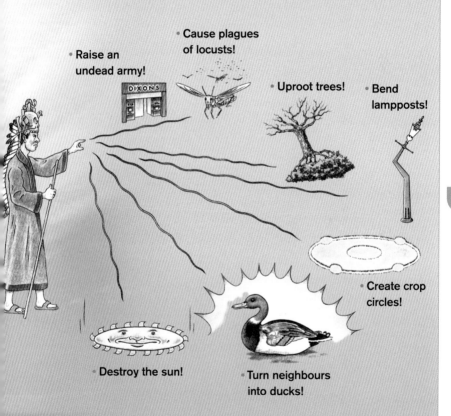

Cursed Headdress of Perzang £199.99

Caution: prolonged use of headdress may cause widespread pestilence and death of first-born son for subsequent family generations.

Unnovations

Order form ▶

Step 1 ▶

Please circle your preferred title and fill out name and address details

Mr ☐   Mrs ☐   Ms ☐   The Late ☐   Captain ☐

First name |

Surname |

Address |

Postcode |

Daytime telephone no.

Evening telephone no.

PIN number

Number you first thought of

Date of birth

Favourite Womble

Price of fame   £

"Goodness me", exclaimed Rosy Wogan the dairymaid, "I've been milking this cow for over two hours and I've only just found out it's a _____".

Email address

Blood type

DNA structure

Worst nightmare

Step 2 ▶

Fill in product details and total up price. And for God's sake do it properly.

PAGE	CATALOGUE No.				PRODUCT	OPTIONS	REALLY?	GIFT-WRAPPED	QTY	PRICE	PRICE AGAIN	MORE PRICE	TOTAL
												Total:	

We use your information to open and run your account, administer prize draws, and for marketing and harassment purposes. We will share your information with retailers from around the world via a bewilderingly sophisticated network of computers that can transmit every conceivable detail about you and your life across continents and oceans so quickly it would make your fucking head spin around like a high-speed rotor. These third-parties will contact you through every possible means of communication, around the clock, 24 hours a day for the rest of your life. And don't think death will let you off the hook either – they'll start bombarding your grieving relatives with leaflets, emails, telephone calls and door-to-door salesmen the moment that coffin lid slams shut, then use a professional medium to contact you in the afterlife and start persuading you to buy windows, or stairlifts, or aftershave, or whatever the heck else it is they're hawking. If you do not wish this not to unhappen, please tick this box []. We routinely monitor and record telephone calls our staff make and receive to ensure you are pestered as efficiently as possible, and because our managing director gets off on sitting behind his desk anally masturbating with a gold-plated fountain pen while listening to tapes of gullible cadavers-in-waiting like you being sold shit by our crack team of underpaid telesales girls, every single one of whom he's fucked for pennies in the stockroom. Really. He went in the back room and stuck it right up them. All the way up. *All the way up their furry little post-pubescent holes.*

Step 3 ▶ Method of Payment
Choose payment method and fill in details

Issue no.

☐ A. By credit / debit card | | | | | | | | | | | | | | | | | |

☐ B. By cheque

☐ C. By sacrifice of first-born

Now sign here
Come on, sign. That's it. Put the pen on the paper and write your fucking name.

Gawp, eat, grin, shit and sleep, knowing you need never have a single thought again

As complex human beings we're continually required to think. Why am I here? Do I want fish? Is it warm enough to go outside without a jumper? The fact is, thinking makes us tired and frequently leads to feelings of confusion, alienation, frustration, anger and despair. Particularly when we're not very good at it. What's the solution? Don't even think about it, because we've thought about it for you, and can say with complete assurance that this is it. What? There you go again. Now stop. Okay? Okay. Good. Meet Thunky-Think-Thinknomore-Thunkishere mittens.

These revolutionary mittens, developed by five of the greatest minds ever to grace the halls of Ipswich Technical College, are pre-programmed with over 6 million thoughts. To operate, simply charge the mittens overnight in our special charger, then in the morning carefully slide a hand inside each mitten and hold your gloved digits before our state-of-the-art Thunky-Think mirror. Within seconds, a message will be spelled across its surface, telling you exactly what to think. No questions. Do I really need the Thunky-Think-Thinknomore-Thunkishere mittens? If you had a pair already, you wouldn't need to ask!

Thunky-Think-Thinknomore-Thunkishere Mitten and Mirror Kit £299.99

I hate women

Other phrases include:
I am a good dancer
I like the Euro
Hanging is good
Buy a bigger fridge

Fun + leisure

All work and no play makes Jack a dull boy. And play won't exactly brighten the little cunt up either – unless, of course, he's been browsing through the following pages of our catalogue.

You're about to feast your eyes on some of the most joy-crammed funjects the human mind could contemplate. Unbridled enjoyment is the aim, and we're sure you won't be disappointed. Because let's face it, one day you're going to die. Alone. Alone and in miserable pain. Scratching at the starched sheets of your deathbed, gargling on your own blood, surrounded by relatives who never liked you anyway, your mind spiralling into pain-induced dementia – and the sole crumb of comfort will be the knowledge that once upon a time, you spent a carefree afternoon chuckling over one of these fabulous products. So buy them.

Because time's running out.

Glasgow's more fun when it's populated by ants

AntGlasgow (page 42)

The ultimate football fan's kit!

Football! It's the beautiful game in which men kick a glorious football around a brilliant field. Football! It's the only thing in the world that never ever gets boring. Football! Despite the blanket TV and press coverage, books, radio phone-ins, pub screenings and widespread football-centric conversation between football-loving chums and strangers, it somehow never loses its magic, especially if you're simple.

But sometimes football isn't quite overpoweringly omnipresent enough. It's a wretched truth that even the most committed football-liking cunt can find themselves spending seconds, minutes – sometimes even hours – adrift in a football-free environment. Perhaps the sport section's missing from your Sunday paper. Or maybe you're stuck in a train carriage struggling to make polite conversation with someone who *thinks* they don't like football.

Prevent the ultimate nightmare happening to you by buying the Footballing World of Soccer Football – the ultimate football fan's kit! There's no better way to express your love of the world's number one sport involving a football.

Ultimate Football Lover's Kit £1999.99

Just look at what each kit contains...

The Big Book of Football Facts

An exclusive 850-page compilation of footballing facts and figures from around the world – which is spherical, just like a football.

The Big Book of Football Facts II

Enjoy your favourite facts all over again! From the people who brought you The Big Book of Football Facts comes a second edition, containing precisely the same compelling footballing facts as the first book, but listed in a slightly different order. *Goal!*

The Third Big Book of Football Facts

The latest instalment in The Big Book of Football Facts series! This third volume includes all the familiar facts you've come to know and love, this time printed in different fonts, and in colour. It's football fact heaven! *Football!*

Matchbag

We've all been there: you're in the middle of watching the big match when nature calls. But the moment you nip to the toilet, in slams the goal of a lifetime! With the Matchbag portable toilet system, such inconvenience need never rear its ugly head again. Simply connect the rubber bag to your penis and anus with the pliable nozzles provided, and hey presto: now you can shit and piss yourself without leaving your seat – and if a rival supporter walks by, you can always burst it in their face, then kick them in the stomach and stab them and call them a cunt. It's the *beautiful game! It's football!*

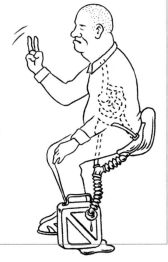

Soccer Action Magnifying Glass

Can't get enough football, even when you're already watching it? Here's the solution: a powerful magnifying lens that lets you watch televised football matches in even more meticulous detail than ever before.

The Best of Post-Match Analysis

At last available on DVD: twenty solid hours of the finest post-match analysis ever broadcast. Also contains additional commentary on the analysis itself, twelve animated diagrams, and a special five-minute break in-between sentences so you can sit in your chair tugging yourself into a sock while thinking about football.

Newspaper Stripping Machine

Destroy all non-football-related newspaper stories with this handy shredding machine! Simply feed your newspaper into the device, switch on and relax as it methodically strips away any and all words not relating directly to the cherished sport. Never again will you have to flip through a dull report on the latest Middle East atrocity in search of the up-to-date football reportage – simply plop open your paper and it's football, football, football all the way! *Hooray for football!*

DULLNEWS

Edible Football Invented

Football Focus – Pages 2,3,4,6,5-40

Fantasy Commentary: the Ultimate Collection

Motty Sprakel

15 hours of inane babble

Fifteen-CD box set containing audio descriptions of imaginary football matches, read by John Motson wearing a football-shaped hat and sitting on a football in the middle of a goal.

Match Projector

Stuck in conversation with a non-football fan? This handy projection kit will beam up to eighteen minutes of pre-recorded match action onto the forehead of anyone standing in front of you. Now you don't need to merely pretend to be interested – you can retain eye contact without twitching nervously and thinking about goals. *Football is the greatest!*

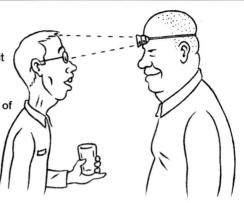

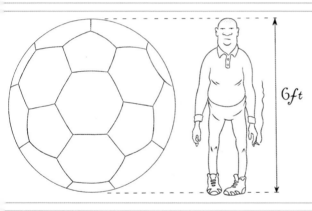

6ft

Giant Football

Ever wanted a football as big as a man? Now you have one. It's a football that's as big as a man. A football as big as a man? That's one big football – *as big as a man!*

Clay Head

Sometimes there's no-one within earshot to discuss football with. Never mind – we've included this speechless clay head in your kit! Simply prop it up on a table or shelf and you can conduct hours of football-centric conversation without fear of interruption or complaint. Talk tactics, reminisce about favourite goals, or swap gossip over upcoming transfers – the choice is both endless and yours.

Glasgow's more fun when it's populated by ants

Ants! With their tiny black heads and twitching antennae, they're dear to all our hearts. But keeping them as pets in the home has always been fraught with disappointment: traditional ant farms are characterless Perspex shells, more akin to a bleak futuristic prison than a comfortable domicile.

Ant Glasgow™ is the answer. A painstakingly-rendered scale model of Scotland's second city, it's the perfect habitat for these loveable insects. You'll take delight in watching them settle into the towerblocks and tenements, scurrying between off-licence and betting shop, just like real Scotsmen! Or why not recreate a terrifying cataclysm by filling the streets with molten chocolate and watching them run for their lives? Your choices, provided they involve ants and cities, are limitless.

Also available:

Dunstable, Rochester, Didcot, Gateshead and Rugby.

Ant Glasgow £599.99

The light, musical alternative to a fuck

The time is right, the wine is sweet, the musky, mildewy odour of sexual arousal is in the air. Normally you'd take the opportunity to make love to one another. But what if you can't? Maybe she's not on the pill, maybe you don't have any rubber johnnies, maybe getting a coil fitted simply isn't appropriate at this stage of the evening. Or maybe it's fear? Fear of failure, fear of disease, fear of prosecution, fear of what God will think when he sees you with his big beady eyes. And he will see you, make no mistake of that.

Whatever the reason, at last there's a safe, painless way to prevent mindless, hedonistic intercourse: Aural Contraceptive. You'll find it impossible to perform any kind of sexual act while listening to this compilation of tracks designed to bring love-making to an abrupt, deflated halt.

Aural Contraceptive includes 3 CDs full of music that you just can't fuck to, including:

The Deadwood Stage – Doris Day
Gotta Get Through This – Daniel Bedingfield
Snooker Loopy – Chas 'n' Dave
Brothers in Arms – Dire Straits
Me Julie – Ali G and Shaggy
Theme from Roobarb
Twistin' By the Pool – Dire Straits
Belfast Child – Simple Minds
Free Nelson Mandela – Special AKA
We Built This City – Starship
It's Horrible Being In Love When You're Eight and a Half – Claire and Friends
On Ilkley Moor Baht'At – Mike Sammes Singers
Barcelona – Freddie Mercury
Theme from Steptoe and Son
Let it Be – Ferry Aid
Paranoid Android – Radiohead
Like Driving in my Car – Madness
Maxwell's Silver Hammer – The Beatles
Mad World – Tears For Fears

The Riddle – Nik Kershaw
Your Mother Should Know – The Beatles
Killing An Arab – The Cure
Xanadu – Olivia Newton John
Birdhouse In Your Soul – They Might Be Giants
The Race – Yello
Meat is Murder – The Smiths
Russians – Sting
The Young New Mexican Puppeteer – Tom Jones
Dancing in the Moonlight – Toploader

Aural Contraceptive £34.99

Frozen piss popsicle sword kit lets bored children hack boredom and playmates to pieces

All children are intrinsically loveable, but as any parent knows, they can also be a monumental headache. Few things grate as much as a bored, restless tot moping around your house in an almighty sulk, whinging and knocking things over until you seriously consider unscrewing the Johnnie Walker and letting the world go and fuck itself to hell.

Occupy their dwarfish minds with this set of plastic sword-shaped ice moulds that provides hours of fun for a few stupid pounds. Kids simply fill the moulds with urine, pop them in the freezer for an hour, and half an hour of Pokemon later – bingo! A set of glinting, sunset-tinted piss swords, ideal for an afternoon of happy garden swashbuckling.

Each sword will last for up to twenty minutes – or far longer in winter – and is guaranteed razor-sharp. And since urine is essentially sterile, infected wounds are a rarity! *Deluxe kit includes sword-fighting video and extra moulds for Shit Cudgels and Puke Bullets.*

Frozen Piss Popsicle Sword Kit £19.99

The easy-seal storage container system that makes desiccated trophies a thing of the past

It's a situation any serial murderer will be familiar with: having stalked and slain your latest victim, you're anxious for a souvenir. Usually this entails hurriedly carving out a selection of organs, stuffing them into a shoebox and storing it under your bed for later use. But all too often, by the time you've acquired sufficient mementos to sew into a necklace and model beneath the moonlight, desiccation sets in – leaving hearts like withered sundried tomatoes and a vulva collection more akin to a range of avant-garde leatherette purses than the display of cherished keepsakes you'd always dreamed of.

TrophyFresh Containers are the first storage vessels designed to meet the needs of the dedicated organ collector. Combining a fingerprint-resistant exterior, an antibacterial Stench Reduction glaze, storage capacity for up to thirteen livers, and an easy-seal lid that makes spillage a rarity even when you're dancing, laughing, and shaking it about like a maraca, they're the solution to any hoarder's woes. All this – plus they're freezer-proof and microwave-friendly to boot!

TrophyFresh Container £3.99

Get those ugly pounds kicked off

In these days of junk food, remote controls and comfortable seating, most of us could do with losing a little weight. Regular exercise is the traditional answer – but unfortunately the vast majority of gymnasiums are pricey, under-equipped and packed with smuggos in leisure gear scuttling about on treadmills in the vain belief it'll render them immortal.

Recent scientific research shows that the most effective way to burn calories isn't lifting weights or dancing on a crash mat, but receiving a severe kicking from an assailant. Not only does the assault itself help break down fat deposits stored inside bones and vital organs, the accompanying rush of fear-stoked adrenalin increases your metabolic rate to previously unattainable levels – so much so, it would be possible to eat a slab of deep-fried cheese the size of a patio door without gaining an ounce of flab to show for it, assuming your jaw hasn't been broken during the attack, which would be a good thing in itself when you think about it.

The KickMaestro Plus lets you experience the miracle of kicking in your own home. Consisting of two robotic legs clad in heavy toe-capped boots, the KickMaestro Plus will boot you around like a sack of old rice, providing fat-blasting hoofs to the head, face and chest at a rate of twenty eight kicks per minute. And unlike a human assailant, the KickMaestro Plus knows no mercy, giving you a workout that's as effective as it is life-threatening.

KickMaestro Plus £199.99

Got a question? Robin knows the answer!

When was Mussolini born? Robin knows! What's the difference between a violin and a viola? Robin knows! What's the Greek word for "ladder"? Robin knows! If you drained a cat of all its blood, how many pint glasses could you fill? Robin knows! All these questions plus one more, answered by a lisping man called Robin. *Available on CD-ROM, VHS, DVD, Braille napkin, and a sheet of A4 paper with biro on it.*

Robin Knows £38.99

Flying onion-and-sock squadron keeps mewling kids out of your hair for a second

Every parent knows what a gigantic pain in the face children can be. Careering around like speed-addled retards one minute, bawling helplessly for your assistance the next. Short of sewing their yelping mouths shut, buying them toys is your only chance of getting a moment's peace.

You may as well buy them this – it's a set of three remote-controlled flying onions with socks hanging off the bottom. They're probably some kind of TV tie-in or something – we neither know nor care. All we know is that they were sodding cheap, and we've got a warehouse full of the things. *So buy them.*

Onion Sock Patrol £999.99

Enjoy raunchy all-American fun wherever you go – with Frat Specs!

Searching for an easy way to brighten your existence?
Here it is: a unique pair of specially-treated wraparound
sunglasses that give the
wearer the impression they
are peering through a hole
into a women's shower room,
just like that bit in "Porky's".

*Other models available
include:*

- Being chased around
  campus by the Dean
- Canteen food fight
- Substituting the college flag for
  a jock strap during an important
  ceremony attended by overseas dignitaries
- Cow tipping
- Cheerleader's bra and panties torn
  off by vacuum cleaner

- Backseat drive-in molestation
- Beta Kappa Omega Delta toga
  party (whatever the fuck that is)
- Stoned swearing parrot landing
  on sheriff's hat

Frat Specs £299.99

Is this the world's most escapade-compatible rope?

Move over, Indiana Jones! With a length of Adventuriser Rope, you can embark on
literally any adventure you care to imagine. Climb cliffs to discover ancient Mayan
treasures, swing across canyons in order to evade blowpipe-toting natives,
or simply hang yourself from a ceiling rafter and explore the mysteries
of the afterlife. The choice is yours!

- Can also be attached to anchors and
  tossed overboard by a
  horny-handed seadog

Adventuriser Rope £499.99

Who hasn't wanted to kill a man?

Life. You've got it. Now you can take it away – and not face immediate vilification or imprisonment. Shooting, strangling, suffocation – the choice is yours. And it needn't cost a fortune.

Most people, at one time or another, have dreamed of killing a man. But as exciting and socially beneficial as it can be, homicide is still considered a crime in most countries. Strange as it may seem, the white-hot thrill of crushing the life from another human remains the preserve of the criminal – ironically, the very people who deserve to be shot in the head. Or strangled. Or drowned until their ears pop and bleed.

But now at last, you can kill and avoid prosecution or guilt with MurderMatchMaker – the unique personalised service that links up those who want to kill with depressives, invalids, incurables, losers and miseries who actually want to be killed. MurderMatchMaker handles everything, from arranging the rendezvous, preparing the paperwork and clearing up afterwards. These are people with a desperate desire to die, allowing you to kill while simultaneously occupying the ethical, legal and moral high ground*.

For a small additional fee, MurderMatchMaker can arrange for your slaying to take place in a range of exciting scenarios. Who could resist striking down a manic-depressive in bed with your partner? Or hacking up a trouble-making Hepatitis C sufferer in a bar? So come on, grab a piece of the action and spill a little blood. You'll never be short of an after-dinner anecdote again.

MurderMatchMaker £599.00

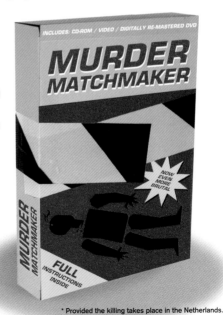

fun & leisure

49

* Provided the killing takes place in the Netherlands.

Perk up your senseless rampage with the world's first massacre soundtrack compilation

Mercilessly gunning down co-workers and acquaintances is the cool craze that's sweeping America – but until now real-life massacres have paled in comparison to the big budget shootouts of silver screen blockbusters such as "The Matrix" and "Mission Impossible II". The reason? The lack of an exciting musical soundtrack to drive the action on.

Now melodically-challenged mass slayings are a thing of the past thanks to "Going Loco" – the world's first compilation album specifically designed to enhance the bloodbath experience. Comprising three CDs packed with carefully-selected tracks that chart a delicate musical path from tense pre-incident build-up to violent carnage to mournful bitter aftermath, "Going Loco" will help you turn an everyday office-bound cull into a professionally orchestrated, ultra-cathartic event to remember for decades to come.

Going Loco Massacre Compilation Album £29.99

CD One: Preparation

Psych yourself up for your orgy of violence with a selection of tunes
designed to set your trigger finger itchin'!

CD ONE CONTAINS:

Phil Collins – In the Air Tonight
Pink Floyd – Another Brick in the Wall
Berlin Philharmonic Orchestra – Also Sprach Zarathustra
The Beatles – Piggies
Matt Munro – Mack the Knife
Original Broadway Cast – Jesus Christ Superstar
Irene Cara – Fame
Boomtown Rats – I Don't Like Mondays
Michael Bolton – When I'm Back On My Feet Again
Chumbawumba – Tubthumping
Police – Every Breath You Take
Blur – There's No Other Way
Buck's Fizz – Making Your Mind Up
Elton John – Saturday Night's Alright for Fighting
Rolling Stones – Paint it Black
M.A.R.R.S – Pump Up the Volume
Super Furry Animals – The Man Don't Give a Fuck
Michael Jackson – Bad
Queens of the Stone Age – Feelgood Hit of the Summer
… and many more

CD Two: In The Thick Of It

Toe-tappin' hits to accompany the sight of
empty shells and spinning, leaking co-workers

CD TWO CONTAINS:

Malcolm Lockyer Orchestra – Theme from The Sweeney
Berlin Philharmonic Orchestra – Ride of the Valkyries
Stakker– Stakker Humanoid
Rage Against the Machine – Killing in the Name Of
Motorhead – Ace of Spades
Survivor – Eye of the Tiger
Spiller – If This Ain't Love
Billy Joel – Uptown Girl
Earth Wind and Fire – Boogie Wonderland
New Kids on the Block – Hangin' Tough
Kiss – Crazy Nights
Queen – Don't Stop Me Now
Bobby Pickett – The Monster Mash
John Denver – Annie's Song
Cher – Gypsies, Tramps, and Thieves
Livin' Joy – Don't Stop Movin'
Anti-Nowhere League – So What?
Joe Dolce – Shaddap Your Face
Ray Parker, Jr – Ghostbusters
Sex Pistols – Bodies
Britney Spears – Oops I Did it Again
Three Tenors – Nessun Dorma
Martine McCutcheon – Perfect Moment
… and many more

CD Three: Aftermath

Pluck up the courage to end it all while the
police surround the building with these
evocative classics

CD THREE CONTAINS:

Judy Collins – Send in the Clowns
Terry Jacks – Seasons in the Sun
Kids from Fame – Starmaker
Neil Diamond – Love on the Rocks
Dan Hill – Sometimes When We Touch
Morris Albert – Feelings
Nick Berry – Every Loser Wins
Grandaddy – So You'll Aim Toward the Sky
Blur – To The End
Don McClean – Vincent
Berlin Philharmonic Orchestra – Beethoven's Seventh
Symphony (Second Movement)
Robbie Williams – Millennium
Johnny Cash – 25 Minutes To Go
R. Kelly – I Believe I Can Fly
Radiohead – Exit Music
Tom Jones - Delilah
Frank Sinatra – It Was a Very Good Year
Edith Piaf – Je Ne Regrette Rien
… and many more

Now you can enjoy some of the aspects of "Carlito's Way" – whatever the weather!

Most people have put Brian De Palma's 1993 gangster blockbuster to the back of their minds, but thankfully not the designers of this fabulous, 100% unofficial piece of garden furniture: a 4m x 3m easily-erected waterproof nylon garden canopy featuring images and words from the movie "Carlito's Way". Now you can be in the movie, in the garden, come rain or shine or hail or snow or wind or hail or rain again.

Other 100% unofficial* movie gazebos available include:

- From Hell
- Whiskey Galore!
- Bend It Like Beckham
- The Parallax View
- Hook
- Straw Dogs

- Three Ninjas Strike Back
- Capricorn One
- Island of Death
- Cool Runnings
- Nic Roeg's Insignificance

* The above items are 100% unofficial and are in no way endorsed by film studios, distributors, cast, crew, gaffers, best boys, the man who does voiceovers for trailers, popcorn stand attendants, video libraries, or Sir Anthony Hopkins.

100% Unofficial "Carlito's Way" Gazebo £99.99

Your lifelong quest for a loyal, compatible sex partner has come to an end

Love, when we encounter it, is the most precious feeling a person can experience. The comforting sensation of brushing against the skin of a person who shares our hopes and dreams, our secret fears and our most heartfelt desires. It is, without question, truly spell-binding. And now you can experience it in the shape of a pig that you fuck.

Each KissMammal 2003 is tailored to your needs by splicing your DNA with that of a smooth, compliant pig – creating a willing sex partner bearing your features. You'll truly feel like you have something in common with the grotesque biological aberration you're entering. Especially when you simultaneously watch its eerily familiar face in a mirror.

Complete with six rear-mounted orifices, and an encyclopaedic knowledge of sexual practices from around the globe, from fellatio to shit-blistering, the KissMammal 2003 will satisfy your every desire – then lick your face clean, a bit like a dog. A dog you've just fucked. And it's hygienic too – while you drift away to empty-bollocked dreamworld, it quietly weeps itself clean with Germolene tears.

KissMammal 2003 £1999.99

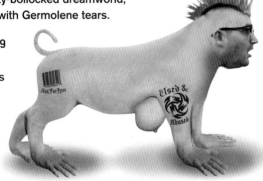

- Now available with breasts
- Fully tattooable and pierceable skin
- Deluxe version has full software support and range of wigs

An orifice for every occasion!

Each KissMammal comes complete with six rear-mounted orifices – a mouth, vagina, anus, and three specially-designed fantasy orifices, created in our laboratories by penile sensation technicians. So whatever your mood, you'll find the port in a storm to accompany it…

Mouth

The KissMammal is skilled in the art of fellatio, using techniques passed down through the ages by traditional Oriental geisha girls and fifteen sailors from Crewe. Its retractable teeth enable it to send shivers down your spine with a playful nibble of your glans one minute, then give you the denture-free suck of a lifetime the next. Each KissMammal's tongue is three times more flexible and far, far stronger than the human equivalent – you can even arm-wrestle against it if you choose! And rest assured, the moment your sphincter-quivering climax arrives, the hungry KissMammal will guzzle down every last drop of semen as though its throat depended on it.

Vagina

"Nothing could be finer / than a pigbeast's wet vagina", Cole Porter once nearly wrote… and we couldn't agree more! The KissMammal's most "traditional" orifice, this deluxe vagina is a precise replica of one belonging to an attractive eighteen-year-old arts student from Milwaukee, and is kept permanently moist thanks to a clever internal network of sophisticated cuntjuice sluicers (patent pending). A fantastic little package, topped off by the pubic goatee of your choice (choose from *Normal, Brazilian, Recently Shaved*, or the daringly retro *1974 Hairburst Naturele*).

Anus

The "forbidden fruit" of the orifice world, the anus is often out of bounds as far as human lovers are concerned. Not so with the KissMammal, which will never complain, no matter how hard or deep you thrust (although repeated use might cause the creature to faint momentarily). As an added bonus, the KissMammal's anus is not used for defecating at all, meaning your penis will smell button-fresh even after an entire afternoon of remorseless sodomy.

Fantasy Orifice #1

Ever wondered how it would feel to fuck a bagful of tongues? Wonder no more! The first of the KissMammal's custom orifices is an inviting cave filled with twenty-eight miniature tongues, each more hungry for bachelor dick than the last.

"Like being fellated by an entire youth orchestra… I must've shot gallons into it."

– BioBoner Review

Fantasy Orifice #2

Hang on tight for the ride of your life! The second fantasy orifice comprises a corkscrew-shaped tunnel lined with undulating muscles, which will suck your penis inside and lead it through a twisting world of ecstasy. Your glans won't know whether it's coming or going as it fires cum in sixteen directions at once. Available in clockwise or anti-clockwise dimensions.

Fantasy Orifice #3

The ultimate in manufactured hole technology, and a scrotum-draining experience you'll never forget. Slide your twitching bone inside Fantasy Orifice 3 and relax as a fully-functioning hand made of warm, wet liver grasps your penis and manually tugs it to climax against a genuine human tit, while six individual sets of lips caress the shaft and a lizardlike tongue emerges from below to lick your balls and anus as clean as Royal kitchenware.

"Left me unable to walk… indescribable… I divorced my wife immediately."

– Demented Thingplugger Illustrated

fun & leisure

55

Cheat on your partner with a clear conscience

A long-term relationship has its rewards, but also several drawbacks. On the one hand, there's security and deep, unquestioning love. On the other, the monotony of seeing the same saggy old arse clambering out of bed every morning. Meanwhile, temptation is everywhere, in the form of flirtatious relationships with attractive co-workers, chance encounters with strangers, and lengthy cyber-wanks with semi-anonymous divorcees from Wisconsin. Everyone longs to savour the joys of a different physical fruit, but the accompanying remorse can be mind-crushing.

Not any more! With the No More Scruples Adultery Mask, even the most sordid two-timing contains up to 76% less guilt than usual. Simply send us a photograph of your beloved, and two weeks later you'll receive a realistic latex mask that authentically replicates their face. Slip it over the head of your illicit lover, and make merry hell in the bedroom, safe in the knowledge that each time you catch their eye, you'll see the face of your loyal partner gazing back – so no matter how stained those hotel bedspreads get, your conscience remains as spotless as ever.

Note: due to recent changes in social toleration, we are no longer able to offer child-sized masks.

No More Scruples Adultery Mask £49.99

House + garden

An Englishman's home is his castle. A Frenchman's home is his maison. But whatever language you're speaking, you're sure to agree that the following articles are truly magnifique.

Whether intended for the kitchen, the bathroom, the cupboard under the stairs, or the dark patch of soil by the pear tree, the booty you'll spy o'er the next few sheets of paper is sure to improve your living standards by a minimum – yes minimum – of 8000% percent.

The other houses in your neighbourhood will start to resemble loveless husks of shit the moment your delivery arrives. And we're so confident you'll be fully satisfied with your purchase, we'll REFUND YOUR MONEY if you can prove otherwise under oath in a court of law, being quizzed by a hotshot lawyer who shits more money in an afternoon than your entire family tree makes in a decade.

Happy house-make-good-ing!

Torture potato-based serfs in the comfort of your own kitchen!

Medieval Potato Catastrophe
(page 59)

Experience a poignant glimpse of unattainable happiness while heating joyless slop

Calling all bachelors! Here's how to enliven those desolate moments spent preparing ready-made meals for one in the kitchen – with the MarriedBliss® Microcook, the world's most moving kitchen appliance. Along with all the handy features you'd expect of a top-of-the-range microwave, the Microcook's front door panel incorporates a full-colour holographic display that projects haunting, ever-shifting images of the idyllic wedding ceremony you will never, ever experience.

As the Microcook blasts your food, the door-bound image flickers: you and a beautiful bride, gently revolving on a starlit dancefloor to the delicate lilt of a romantic medley, your face aglow with triumphant pride while your betrothed gazes at you with eyes full of love. It's a vision of hypnotic joy – until the door abruptly springs open with a piercing electronic beep, revealing a bleak plastic trayful of overheated swill, ideal for forking dolefully into a downturned mouth between guttural sobs of wounded despair.

MarriedBliss® Microcook Oven
£99.99

The potato-based atrocity that's fun to make and eat!

Deep-fried potato chips. They're as much a part of British tradition as bangers and mash, real ale and heart disease. Usually, preparing and cooking chips is a crashingly mundane task – skinning potatoes, slicing them into shape, heating the oil… I mean, fucking hell.

Liven up the cooking process with Medieval Potato Catastrophe™– the fun kitchenware playset that turns ordinary chip-frying into a public execution straight out of the Dark Ages. First use the tiny people-shaped cutters to carve your potatoes into pleasing humanoid shapes – serfs, peasants, and the occasional bewildered knave. Then don your executioner's mask and feel the leer spread across your face as you dip your helpless carbohydrate victims into the bubbling oil. *Order now and receive a FREE suspected witch ducking stool fondue set!*

Medieval Potato Catastrophe™ – £79.99

house & garden

59

Got a car? Get a Car Hat™

So you've bought your first motor car, fitted it with a brand new FM/AM stereo player, and put brand new covers on the seats. But it isn't quite enough, is it? What you need is Car Hat™, the must-have motor accessory that all motorists must have. Available in two distinct styles (top hat and Busby), Car Hat™ is the only hat available that's directly marketed at car drivers (people who drive cars). Wear Car Hat™ in traffic jams, during long drives in the country or even while you're watching TV at home. It doesn't matter. It really doesn't. It's just a hat.

Car Hat™: £59.99

Are these the world's most harrowing plates?

In today's image-obsessed society everyone knows the benefits of keeping trim. Heart attacks, diabetes, bleeding rolls of pus-filled fat hanging from unloved thighs – all a product of over-eating. And as everyone knows, fat people are an offence.

So at last there's good news for would-be dieters, with the BleakEat Easy-Slim Plate Collection. Each one comes decorated with a picture so stomach-churningly repulsive you'll leave meals unfinished just to avoid a glimpse of the vile image lurking on the platter below. Available in three distinctive ranges – Nuclear Holocaust, The Starving and Anal Maladies – these unique crockery creations are as morally reprehensible as they are dishwasher proof. Could YOU spoon warm peas off the face of a starving child? Try it. Go on. *Try.*

BleakEat Easy-Slim Plates £29.99 each

HOLO-CAUST!

THE STARVING!

ANAL MALADIES!

The mouthless stumbling boy creature that shakes illegal intruders to the very core

Once a burglar has targeted your property, there's little you can do to stop him. Locks and chains may stave off the inevitable break-in for a few minutes, but before long he's in: scurrying through your house like an overgrown rat on a scavenger hunt, stuffing jewellery and valuables into his holdall, pocketing your passport and ejaculating into your underwear drawer. It's time to teach him a lesson – a lesson he'll never forget.

This mouthless, stumbling toddler has been grown in a petri dish by madmen. It doesn't need food or water: it lives for ninety days before quietly withering away to a husk. But until then it will stand silently in the corner of your living room, shuddering and shaking, emitting muffled groaning sounds and gently bumping its head against the wall. You'll get used to it after a couple of hours – but a burglar encountering it unexpectedly will have his brain dented for years. In fact it's guaranteed to leave intruders in need of psychiatric treatment for a minimum of six months. But please order soon – we've got a warehouse full of them, and to be honest they're doing our heads in.

Stumbleboy £899.99

Let The Alan Collection bring a vague sense of purpose and 3000 Alans to your desultory life

Ladies! In the flower of youth, your life's a twirling chucklebox of parties, whispers, kisses and song. It's perfume and skirts, flat pints of cider, and "Fat Bottomed Girls" on the jukebox while your boyfriend pots the black. Then you age. You settle down. Life and metabolism slow to a crawl. Bored out of your mind, you and a partner breed and spawn; a daughter perchance. You get fat. And what does she do? Mess up in school and smoke out the window and start hanging round with boys bound for Borstal. Just think: one of those Martin Fowler lookalikes may have touched your daughter's mimsy.

Distract yourself by slowly collecting some shit, overpriced rubbish, then displaying it in your gaudy proletarian living room. Fuck, this'll do: a collection of replica heads of men called Alan. We found their faces on the Internet and recreated them in polymer resin. They're not hand-painted: all the features are sprayed on by a gigantic machine. And we absolutely cannot justify the asking price. But what do you care? You're at your wit's end.

The Alan Collection – £34.99 for first Alan, £49.99 for each subsequent Alan

Can't tell your arse from your elbow? Now you can!

Tired of trying to shit through your elbow or bend your arm with your arse? Put an end to arse-elbow mix-up misery with this handy visual guide. Fixes to any wall-like surface, bringing instant arse-elbow anti-confusion to any room in your home. Place it in kitchens, bedrooms, bathrooms, lounges – you can even stick it to a patio door and look at it from the garden. Works in all weather and lighting conditions (except absolute darkness), and is printed on both sides in case you're too bloody stupid to even put it up properly.

Arse-Elbow Confusion Destroyer £27.99

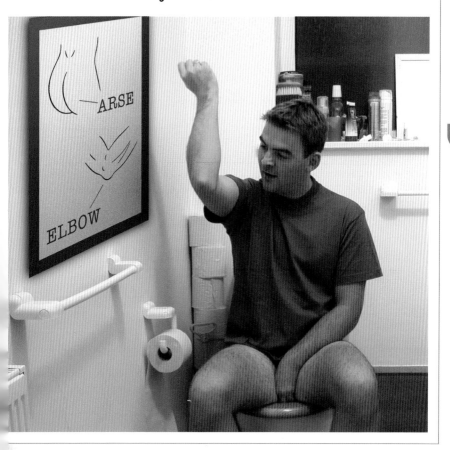

Artist's Impression

Let these acerbic talking bookends pour scorn on your doomed stabs at literary improvement

Who doesn't love a library? With their hushed whispers, mouldy aroma and inert, oppressive air, they turn the potentially carefree pastime of book-browsing into a brain-creasing crawl through a dismal valley of grey authoritarian disapproval. It's easy to imagine a grim-faced Margaret Hamilton lookalike popping up from behind a dusty shelf to clip your eyelids off with a pair of shears, just because you had the audacity to leaf through something by Sven Hassel or stare at an encyclopaedia with a topless tribeswoman in it for eight seconds too long. No wonder reading books is more popular than ever before, especially amongst the young.

It's always been a challenge to recreate that uneasy, judgmental library atmosphere in the comfort of your own slum – but now you can, with the Chastise-a-Synth Bookends; a remarkable pair of dog-shaped lumps that use computerised voice synthesis to mock your choice of book – whatever it may be. Whether you feel like browsing the classics, or nosing into the latest John Grisham, the patent technology will blurt out a withering dismissal the instant you go to pull it from the shelf, leaving you feeling belittled and humiliated – guaranteed! You may never read a book again. If you're lucky.

Chastise-a-Synth Bookends £19.99 (a pair)